ACTON COMMON

GREEN

Acton Common Field

Chiswick Common Field

The Bowling Alley

CHISWICK

HAM

Four Miles from Hyde Park Corner

Windmill Farm

Sneckenhall

TURLINGTON

For Your 50th Birthday
26th August 2014 .

WILD ABOUT
Chiswick

WHERE THE CITY MEETS THE COUNTRY

By Andrew Wilson

Sponsored by

Andrew Nunn & Associates

Chiswick's Leading Independent Estate Agent

I would like to dedicate this book to my family, particularly my wife, who had to bear the brunt of the extra work it took to produce my books this year. Love you xx

Clockwise from top right: Christ Church, Turnham Green; Chiswick Mall; St Michael's Church, Bedford Park; Chiswick House.
The map on the end papers is taken from John Rocque's famous *London Map of 1746*.

Contents

Welcome to Wild About Chiswick

Welcome to my latest collection of photographs. I have many friends in Chiswick and with this in mind and its abundance of places to visit and photograph it was an obvious choice for one of my next books. As it turned out, given the sheer amount of material that I have gathered over the past year, this has turned into my biggest book to date. From the beautiful riverside setting of Strand on the Green all the way to Bedford Park, via Old Chiswick and The Mall, there was no end to the photographic inspiration. As followers of my books will know I do much of my exploring in the company of my springer, Josie, and this new book was so convenient – a quick hop across Barnes Bridge and we were there.

My books take some time and effort to produce but this is no one man (and his dog) show and I would like to take this opportunity to thank a few people for helping me. Firstly, Andrew and Susan Nunn and the staff at local estate agents, Andrew Nunn & Associates and Fuller's Brewery, who have kindly sponsored the book. Andrew has been right behind me ever since I first contacted him earlier in 2013 and as he well knows, I love nothing better than on a fine day taking myself off for a stroll with my camera and it is the financial help of local people like this that make all this possible, so thank you.

I would also like to thank my writer, Andrea Cameron, from The Hounslow and District History Society, who with the sterling help of Tom Sears, have crafted the history pages at the front and the section introductions. Thanks also to Silvina De Vita for her map. Further thanks should go to my designers, Tim and Dan from Ball Design and my great friend and colour printing expert, Paul Sherfield. I may take the pictures but these guys bring them all to life.

My books take well over a year to produce and I meet many people along the way who have helped or contributed and unfortunately space does not allow me to mention you all, so my apologies if I have missed you off, it isn't personal. I have in many cases made reference to people within the relevant text, so if not here, you may well find yourself in the book itself.

With so much to see and record I have left some things untouched, for instance, the playing fields on Dukes Meadows, the other allotments and I would love to have seen the gardens inside the convent in Grove Park to name but a few examples. However, there is only so much space and time in which to do what I do and apologies if you have not made this first edition. I hope you enjoy my latest book; it was just the best fun.

Andrew Wilson
November 2013

Josie, my constant companion, wading at low tide at Chiswick Mall.

First Edition – ©Unity Print and Publishing Limited 2013
Designed by Ball Design Consultancy *www.balldesignconsultancy.com*
Proofread by Tom Sears *www.tom-sears.com*
Printed by Headley Brothers of Ashford, Kent. *www.headley.co.uk*
Bound by Green Street Bindery of Oxford
www.maltbysbookbinders.com
Colour Management by Paul Sherfield of The Missing Horse Consultancy. *www.missinghorsecons.co.uk*
Published by Unity Print and Publishing Limited, 18 Dungarvan Avenue, London SW15 5QU. Tel: +44 (0)20 8487 2199
aw@unity-publishing.co.uk www.unity-publishing.co.uk

Opposite: Christ Church, Turnham Green

Chiswick

A SHORT HISTORY OF THE AREA
by Andrea Cameron

The earliest spelling of Chiswick is *Ceswic*, which is Anglo-Saxon for *cheese farm*. It is thought that Dukes Meadows played host to an annual cheese fair, supported by the surrounding meadows and farms. This bucolic image reminds us that before it became a London suburb in the late 19th century, Chiswick spent centuries as a sleepy riverside Middlesex village.

Chiswick originally consisted of Church Street and Chiswick Mall, to which were added Strand on the Green, Little Sutton, Turnham Green and Stamford Brook. In the second half of the 19th century Grove Park and Bedford Park were developed. Bedford Park is now shared with Ealing andStamford Brook with Hammersmith.

The Domesday Survey of 1086 has no entry for Chiswick, as it was then part of the Manor of Fulham, which belonged to St. Paul's Cathedral. By the 12th century St. Paul's Cathedral owned two manors in Chiswick – Sutton Manor and the Chiswick Prebendal Manor.

Archaeological excavations in the early 19th century showed that there was prehistoric life in Chiswick, both human and animal. A little later, the Romans arrived and built a road from London to the separate kingdom of Wessex. Through Chiswick this became known as the High Road. Anglo-Saxon archaeological finds were of a military nature, showing that their armies subsequently used the road.

Chiswick village grew up around a parish church, established by 1811 and dedicated to St. Nicholas. From the 16th century large country retreats were built along the riverside for wealthy residents. The locals meanwhile lived in a group of cottages around the church known as Slut's Hole and understandably re-christened Fisherman's Place in 1865. Many families earned their living from fishing the River Thames, but by the late 19th century the river had been devastatingly polluted by the discharge of waste. It was impossible to catch enough fish to earn a living. Over the past 25 years the Thames has been cleaned up immeasurably and now teams with life again.

Most forms of transport have served Chiswick at some point or other. The ferry is first mentioned in 1659 but was probably in existence even before then. It crossed the river from the bottom of Chiswick Lane to Barnes. Later it moved closer to St. Nicholas Church and continued to operate until the 1930s.

Chiswick from the air, or at least the 14th floor of the BSI building in Gunnersbury. A huge thanks to Caroline Tyler from BSI for helping set this up and Caroline, Maria and Krystine from Autobar for letting me into their office to admire the view and take some pictures.

In 1933 Chiswick Bridge on the Great Chertsey Road opened. The Roman road became the Stagecoach route to the West Country in the early 18th century, with routes to Bath, Bristol, Exeter, and Truro. In 1784 Mail coaches travelled to Bath and Bristol, taking precedence over the Stagecoaches. By 1832, 22 coaches a day were travelling to Bristol, with the first staging post being Hounslow. The completion of the Great Western Railway from Paddington to Bristol in 1841 led to the closure of the coaching routes to the west.

Local coach services made two journeys a day from Turnham Green to London. By 1845 horse buses travelled to London every 15 minutes. By 1882 horse drawn trams ran to Kew Bridge, and from 1901 to 1935 electric trams ran from Shepherd's Bush to Hounslow. Motor buses appeared in 1911, being opened topped until c.1919, and trolley buses ran on the tram route from 1935 until 1962. The London and South Western Railway line from Waterloo to Hounslow opened in 1849. In 1867 the railway bridge was built across the Thames

at Strand on the Green to take the railway into Richmond from Kensington. This provided a station at Turnham Green.

The largest estate was that of Chiswick House, which passed between wealthy families for over 300 years after its establishment. The first house there, of Jacobean design, was completed c.1610. In 1682 it was sold to the 1st Earl of Burlington and in 1704 was inherited by his great grandson, Richard Boyle, 3rd Earl of Burlington. Richard did the grand tour of Europe and fell in love with the 16th century Palladian villas in northern Italy, designed by Andrea Palladio. He returned to England determined to build the most perfect example of Palladian architecture. Architect Colin Campbell helped his attempt, building Chiswick House c.1727–29, while architect William Kent laid out the grounds. Burlington's daughter married the heir to the Duke of Devonshire and as 4th Duke of Devonshire, Chiswick House passed into his ownership. Georgiana, 5th Duchess of Devonshire, held parties in support of the Whig political party.

In the 1920s, the 9th Duke of Devonshire put the estate up for sale as building land. Brentford and Chiswick Council, Middlesex County Council and architectural historians raised money to purchase the estate. Brentford and Chiswick Urban District Council administered both the house and the grounds. Some blast damage occurred in the Second World War. In the late 1940s the Ministry of Works became responsible for the house and the Council continued to be responsible for the grounds. Today English Heritage owns the house and Hounslow Council with a trust of local representatives maintains the grounds.

Strand on the Green grew up in the Middle Ages as a fishing community. The larger houses were built from the 18th century, and the largest of those is Zoffany House (pictured overleaf), built in 1705, which was home to Bavarian artist Johann Zoffany from the late 18th century until his death in 1811. Oast houses, built in the 19th century, housed hops, barley and malt for local breweries. These were brought from Kent in large Thames sailing barges. 18th century pubs included The City Barge, The Bulls Head, and the 19th century Steam Packet, now a Cafe Rouge restaurant.

Church Street and Chiswick Mall contain buildings from the 16th century. The Old Burlington in Church Street was a pub until c.1917 and is now a private house. Corney House was the home of the 4th Earl of Bedford. Demolished in the early 19th century, it became the site of the Thorneycroft Boatyard from c.1865 to 1904, where ships for the Royal Navy, the French Navy and the Japanese Navy were built. On Chiswick Mall, Walpole House was the home of Barbara Villiers, Duchess of Cleveland, in the 17th century.

Bedford House from c.1945 was the home of the acting Redgrave family. A house in Boston Square is said to have been the site of the school in Vanity Fair. Nearby is Hogarth's House, an early 18th century building, which was the country home of artist, William Hogarth.

In the 1870s Grove Park was developed with large detached Victorian houses. At the same time Bedford Park was planned as the first suburban garden city. The houses were designed in the style of Queen Anne revival and were for rent by artisans. The Irish poet, W.B. Yeats, was an early resident. Bedford Park is shared with L.B. Ealing. East of Bedford Park is Stamford Brook, shared with L.B. Hammersmith and Fulham. Stamford Brook House, which is 17th century with 18th century additions, was the home of artist, Lucien Pissarro in the early 20th century.

Chiswick Ait, is the island in the River Thames, where osiers were grown and harvested, dried, stripped and woven into large baskets by women in their own homes and used in the market gardens. Oliver's Island at Strand on the Green for

The clock on St. Michael's Church in Bedford Park. There to commemorate the first vicar, Harold Wilson.

centuries had a boat building and repair yard. The River Thames besides having the sailing barges, from 1824, had passenger steamers from Queenhithe, near the Tower of London, to Richmond.

By 1900, Turnham Green and Chiswick High Road had become a London suburb. Industry in the form of Chiswick Products which became Reckett and Coleman and the London Transport Chiswick Works for the training of bus drivers and the maintenance of buses opened in the 1930s. Sanderson Wallpaper and Upholstery Company were in Chiswick from 1870 to 1930.

In the Second World War Chiswick suffered bomb damage and in September 1944, the first V2 rocket landed in Staveley Road, killing two people and causing 14 houses to be destroyed.

In 1959 the Hogarth roundabout was built and Hogarth Lane was widened to bring the Cromwell Road extension through Chiswick to the newly built M4 motorway, which went westwards to South Wales.

Chiswick continues to be developed by demolishing, detached Victorian houses with gardens, for the building luxury apartments.

Andrea Cameron is a historian from the Hounslow and District Historical Society. andreacameron@tiscali.co.uk

The then largest house in Strand on the Green, built in the early 18th century, was home to Bavarian artist Johann Zoffany from the late 18th century until his death in 1811.

Chiswick

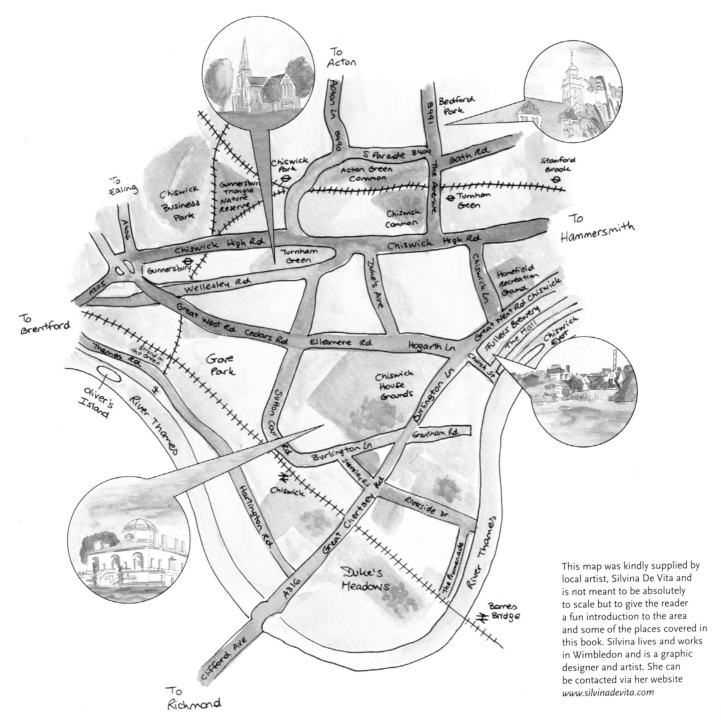

To Acton

To Ealing

To Brentford

To Hammersmith

To Richmond

Bedford Park

Acton Ln B410

S Parade B409

Bath Rd

Stamford Brook

The Avenue

Turnham Green

Chiswick Park

Acton Green Common

Chiswick Common

Gunnersbury Triangle Nature Reserve

Chiswick Business Park

A406

A205

Chiswick High Rd

Chiswick High Rd

Gunnersbury

Turnham Green

Wellesley Rd

Dukes Ave

Chiswick Ln

Homefield Recreation Ground

Great West Rd Chiswick

Fullers Brewery

The Mall

Chiswick Eyot

Great West Rd   Cedars Rd

Ellesmere Rd

Hogarth Ln

Church St

Thames Rd

Strand on the Green

Gore Park

Sutton Court Rd

Chiswick House Grounds

Burlington Ln

Grantham Rd

Oliver's Island

River Thames

Hartington Rd

Chiswick

Staveley Rd

Riverside Dr

River Thames

Great Chertsey Rd

A316

Duke's Meadows

The Promenade

River Thames

Barnes Bridge

Clifford Ave

This map was kindly supplied by local artist, Silvina De Vita and is not meant to be absolutely to scale but to give the reader a fun introduction to the area and some of the places covered in this book. Silvina lives and works in Wimbledon and is a graphic designer and artist. She can be contacted via her website www.silvinadevita.com

9

Old Chiswick
and The Mall

In the 12th century the original riverside village of Chiswick comprised two roads – Church Street and Chiswick Mall. The Thames was the preferred means of transport in medieval and Tudor times, being safer than the highwaymen-infested roads. As a result, royalty floated past Chiswick regularly on their way from London to Richmond and Hampton Court Palaces, and to Windsor Castle. From the 16th century, large detached houses built along Chiswick Mall provided country retreats for the rich and famous. The landscape has changed but the rich and famous are still happily ensconced there today.

Right: Hogarth's House, just off the Great West Road near the roundabout named after him.

Left: The small group of house-boats near St Nicholas Church.

This Page: The Mall from the shore.

Left: One of the large boats moored up all year round.

Right: Many water sports are enjoyed on the Thames, so as well as rowing there are several sailing clubs and also canoeing from the RNLI station on Chiswick Pier, off Corney Reach.

Below: The Mall in winter

Opposite, top: The Mall regularly floods, sometimes cutting off the road completely; doesn't stop a springer wanting to play mind, they love water.

Opposite, bottom: St Nicholas church from the river at dusk.

Overleaf: The river and Chiswick Eyot late one evening in March 2013; terrific light that night.

Top left: Some children playing about on the shore.

Bottom left: The Mall in full autumn colour.

Right: The Mall at low tide.

This page: The Mall and Chiswick Eyot in winter.

This page: The Mall is known for its spectacular display of wisteria and 2013 was no exception.

Opposite: The wonderful magnolia from the garden of Bedford House – many thanks to Sarah for letting me into her lovely garden (see page 210 for more pictures).

This page, top and bottom left: The Mall and the river are a regular draw for walkers.

Bottom right: One of the gardens on the river side of the road has this wonderful sculpture in their garden.

Left: The aptly named Wisteria House in Church Lane.

Right top left: A rather like this ornate urn, which can be found along The Mall.

Right top right: The view towards Hammersmith across one the gardens facing the river.

Bottom left and right: Church Lane.

Fuller's Brewery

In 1845 John Fuller, Henry Smith and John Turner formed their independent brewing company, Fuller, Smith & Turner, which has been brewing beer on the Griffin Brewery site ever since. Remarkably, descendants of each family are still heavily involved with the day-to-day running of the whole operation. Fuller's is probably most famous for its ever-popular, eminently drinkable 'London Pride' ale, which constitutes 75% of their output. The site has been used for brewing for over 350 years, stretching back before the establishment of Fuller's to the era of Oliver Cromwell.

Top left: The brewery was a stopping off point this summer for the inaugural Ride London.

Bottom left: Barrel washing.

Top right: The brewery run tours every day, which take you to the very heart of the process.

Bottom right: Some of the museum pieces the brewery have in their 'Hock Cellar'.

Opposite, top left: The main building is famous for its wisteria, which was badly affected from the storm we had in London in October 1987. Thankfully it has been nursed back to full health.

Opposite, top right: The view of the brewery from the garden of Bedford House on the Mall.

Opposite, bottom right: Entrance to the brewery.

Corney Reach and Regency Quay

Main picture: Corney Reach and Regency Quay one glorious summer's morning.

Inset: The distinctive dome covered in snow at Corney Reach.

Corney Reach is a relatively new development, which was built in the mid '90s. The land had previously been a part of a large house belonging to The Earl of Bedford, before being demolished in 1832 and becoming the famous Thornycroft Boat Yard. With the demand for larger and larger ships Thornycroft was eventually forced to move away to Southampton in 1904, whereupon it was split up into various industrial units before being bombed during the second world war. Thank you to the Chiswick W4 website, from an original work by Gillian Clegg, and the Brentford and Chiswick Local History Society for the background on this.

Right: Chiswick Pier. Completed in 1997 as part of the Corney Reach development, the Chiswick Pier Trust, which manages the moorings, is a charity whose main aim is to promote use of the Thames.

Left bottom: Two of the larger boats moored up on The Pier.

Left: Corney Reach looking West.

Right and overleaf: Corney Reach from the south side of the river in Barnes.

Top left: The RNLI have a station on The Pier, with two boats.

Right and bottom left: Pissarro is a popular restaurant found by The Pier.

Bottom right and opposite: The beautiful spring blossom at Regency Quay.

Grove Park

In the mid 19th century the Duke of Devonshire owned 50% of the land in Chiswick Parish. Chiswick railway station and track were part of his patch, and in 1867 he published plans for an estate between the river and the railway. The Duke paid for the Grove Hotel to be built to attract visitors to Chiswick riverside. The extensive sporting facilities included a putting green, tennis club, cricket pitch and golf course, as well as punting on the lake in Grove Park grounds. The Duke also paid for St. Paul's church to be built in 1873.

Below: Chiswick Bridge from the Thames Bank in Mortlake. Built on the site of a former ferry, Chiswick Bridge was opened in 1933. At the time it had the largest concrete central span of any bridge over the Thames.

Top right: Chiswick Marina

Bottom right: Spring got off to a late and shaky start in 2013, with cold weather persisting well into April – this was the first butterfly I came across during the year, a beautiful Comma at the Marina.

Chiswick Regatta

The Thames is known for its Rowing Regattas, which are run the length and breadth of the river from early spring through summer. The Chiswick Regatta is held each year at The Quintin Boat Club, near Chiswick Bridge, and this year was held at the beginning of May. Thankfully the weather was fine. The Club can trace its history back to the 1880s, well before the bridge arrived and the area was quite rural. My thanks to their captain, Dave King, who kindly gave me some background on the club.

Bottom right: Although I didn't know it at the time, this boat crew from St Paul's School won their category, which was impressive given that they beat several teams supposedly better on paper.

Opposite top left:
Quintin Boat Club.

Opposite top right: One of
the St Paul's crew passing
the finishing post for the
University Boat Race.

Top left: Quintin's Club flag.
Top right: The boat crews
were able to use the field next
to the river to overload all
their gear.

Bottom left: the view from the
club house balcony.

Bottom right: The crews
coming ashore between
races with Mortlake in the
background.

Overleaf: The clouds did
eventually disperse leaving
a nice afternoon for racing.

Opposite and overleaf: Fauconberg Road, Grove Park, where many of the local shops can be found.

This page: Chiswick Park Station; and the 9.15 arriving on platform 1 is the steam train to the coast – I know that quite a few trains come through here but it must still come as a surprise for those waiting for their normal commuter train.

The local shops in Fauconberg Road, Grove Park

This page: Sutton Court, originally the site of Sutton Court House. The current flats date from 1905. According to historian, Andrea Cameron, Sutton Court was one of two manors in Chiswick and can trace its history all the way back to 1181. In an illustrious history, one owner in the 16th century was Sir Thomas More.

This page: Grove Park in spring.

Bottom left: I was pleased to discover this particularly fine white wisteria tree in Burnaby Crescent.

Strand on the Green

Strand on the Green was a settlement by 1400, when it was called Stronde. By 1550 it became Strond and in 1610 Ye Strande. Strand is a bank or shore beside a green place. From the early 18th century the larger houses were built along the riverside. Most of these are still there.

In the mid 18th century they provided homes for courtiers of King George III, including the artist Johan Zoffany. In the 20th century celebrity residents included actress Eileen Atkins, actor Donald Pleasance and TV comedy writer Carla Lane.

Previous page: Kew Railway Bridge

This page: You can get some spectacular sunsets at Strand on the Green, here looking towards Brentford. The swans can look wonderful in the setting sun.

Left: Looking west as the sun goes down.

Right: The towpath at Strand on the Green is a wonderful place to visit, very pretty and with three pubs a nice place to stop and admire the view.

Top: The Thames at low tide.

Bottom: Strand on the Green from Kew Bridge.

Opposite, top left: Annies restaurant, another favourite haunt for locals, here enjoying an early breakfast.

Opposite, bottom: Strand on the Green from the towpath on the south side of the river in Kew.

Opposite, top right: Café Rouge, previously the Steam Packet pub.

Overleaf: Strand on the Green on a misty morning in December 2012.

Top left: The start of the towpath beside the river in Strand on the Green.

Top right: One of the larger houses bordering the river.

Bottom left: One of the more unusual house numbers on Thames Road.

Opposite: Looking west as the sun sets over Brentford.

Grove Park Terrace Street Party. Held each summer, this jolly
event is put on by the residents and helps raise money for local
charities, which this year was the Tommy Hollis Children's
Fund. Tommy Hollis was tragically killed by a falling lamp
post outside Chiswick Town Hall back in 2010. In his memory,
his parents Kate and Chris set up the fund to try to help
other children, either underprivileged, sick or orphaned.

Opposite, top left: Kate and Andrew Nunn take on the onerous
task of trying to judge the cake competition.

Staveley Road is extremely well
known for its stunning display
of cherry blossom in the spring.
Even The Queen has been said
to drive here especially to see
the spectacle. Although delayed
by the weather, this year did
not disappoint.

Another regular charitable event on the Grove Park calender is Grovestock, held at the end of the summer in the grounds of St Pauls Church. This family friendly event was great fun, with all the usual things on offer, cakes and Fuller's beer plus the music of course.

Left: Amongst the musical acts on offer, Money Penny bottom right and a particular favourite of mine, Matt Addy, who delivered a really fine set. As it started to get dark another great act were Taxi Joe, with their good old fashioned blues.

Opposite, bottom right: Helping to make the event a success are on the right, Maria Kempinska from Jongleurs, a local resident, and in the middle, actress Vicki Michelle together with the some local girls and 'Mr Funny' at the back.

Chiswick House

The largest estate in the area was that of Chiswick House, which passed between wealthy families for over 300 years after its establishment. The first house there, of Jacobean design, was completed c.1610. In 1682 it was sold to 1st Earl of Burlington and in 1704 was inherited by his great grandson, Richard Boyle, 3rd Earl of Burlington. Richard did the grand tour of Europe and fell in love with the 16th century Palladian villas in northern Italy, designed by Andrea Palladio. He returned to England determined to build the most perfect example of Palladian architecture. Architect Colin Campbell helped his attempt, building Chiswick House c.1727–29, while architect William Kent laid out the grounds. Burlington's daughter married the heir to the Duke of Devonshire and as 4th Duke of Devonshire, Chiswick House passed into his ownership. Georgiana, 5th Duchess of Devonshire, held parties in support of the Whig political party.

In the 1920s, the 9th Duke of Devonshire, put the estate up for sale as building land. Brentford and Chiswick Council, Middlesex County Council and architectural historians raised money to purchase the estate. Brentford and Chiswick Urban District Council administered both the house and the grounds. Some blast damage occurred in the Second World War. In the late 1940s the Ministry of Works became responsible for the house and the Council continued to be responsible for the grounds, Today English Heritage owns the house and Hounslow Council with a Trust of local representatives maintains the grounds.

Chiswick House in the snow.
The house is in the care of
English Heritage, for which
a big thank you for allowing
me to reproduce the
pictures I have taken –
www.english-heritage.org.uk

Chiswick House looks great whatever the season – autumn.

Right: The newly restored conservatory in the background.

Opposite: The ionic temple
in the background with the
amphitheatre and obelisk
at the front.

Right: In the summer and organised by the Chiswick House Friends was an evening of opera. The Friends were founded in 1984 by local residents and dog-walkers wanting to do something about the general neglect of the gardens and the poor security for visitors. Since the major restoration work in 2010, the Friends have supported the Chiswick House and Gardens Trust who manage the whole estate by helping to raise funds and providing a valuable link between the new Trust and the local community.

www.chfriends.org.uk

The magnificent trees beside the lake in all their autumn splendour.

This was an early season game, possibly their first, back in April 2013. Thankfully the weather had just improved to be more like spring, than the winter-like conditions we had been enduring.

Bedford Park

Bedford Park was planned as the first *'suburban garden city'* in 1875. An 1883 advertisement described it confidently as the *'healthiest place in the world'*. The developer was Jonathon Carr, a property speculator, who employed E.W. Godwin, Norman Shaw, Maurice Adams and others to design houses in the Queen Anne revival style.

St. Michael's church, 1879, was designed by Norman Shaw. The School of Art, 1883, was designed by Maurice Adams. The Bedford Park Club, 1876, also by Shaw, gave the area a sense of self-contained community, as did the Tabard Inn.

In 1967, 356 houses were listed as Grade II and in 1969–70 Bedford Park was made a conservation area.

Bedford Park is known for its beautiful red brick buildings and unusual architecture.

Left: Abinger Road.

Right: Chiswick Court Hotel in Bath Road.

Opposite and top: The house on the corner of Addison Grove has a wonderful Camellia and this year even they were astonished by how prolific it was; possibly down to the strange weather we have been having.

Bottom: A nice feature of Lonsdale Road is the flowers the residents grow around the bases of the trees.

Opposite, top left:
Abinger Road.

Opposite, bottom right and this page: Priory Avenue.

Opposite, bottom left:
South Parade.

Opposite, top right:
Le Vacherin, the French restaurant found on South Parade, opposite Acton Common.

The Bedford Park Festival

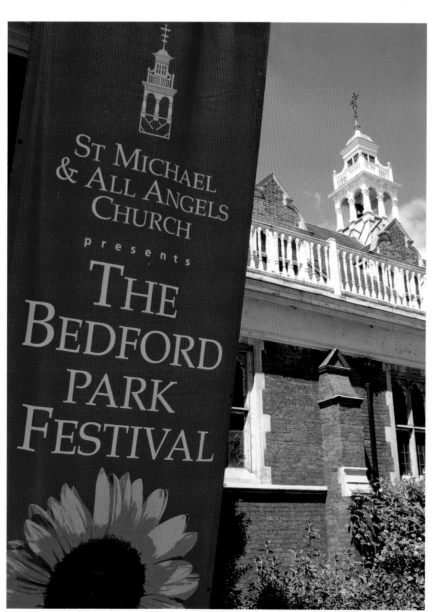

The Bedford Park Festival – this is the main event of the two week festival, the two day fête on Acton Common. This year held on Saturday 8th and Sunday 9th June.

The fête had all the usual attractions, a music tent, games including skittles, local produce, a kids area, food and drink and much more.

No fête is complete without a bit of dressing up to entertain the kids.

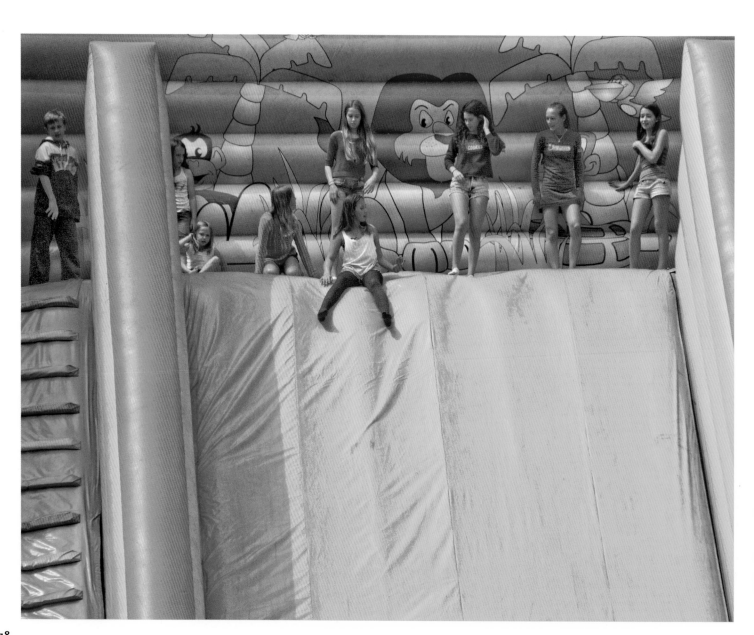

Street Life

Chiswick High Road and Turnham Green Terrace are two of the most vibrant shopping streets to be found in London, and certainly command high rents from shopkeepers. One part of the appeal for many shoppers may be the width of the High Road, which is much wider and more inviting than many high streets. It's interesting to note that the area keeps its buzz despite not having a Town Centre Manager to help coordinate their Christmas lights and other events, as many other London high streets do.

Right: Lovely old cart outside Wheeler's Garden Centre.

Left and bottom:
Dale Street

Right: Murals on
Coombe Road

123

Above: Chiswick Town Hall. The present hall dates from 1901.

Opposite: The alleyways connecting Stamford Brook station from the other parts of Chiswick.

Opposite: Stamford Brook was one of the many tributaries that ran into the Thames from the Chiswick area, all of which by 1900 had been covered over and used as the basis of the local sewer system. Another part of the brook system was used to form the lake at Chiswick House.

This page: Airedale Avenue where you can find The Hogarth Health Club. The land was acquired in 1978 by Colin White and it has remained a family business ever since. Its grand opening was in 1981 and was one of the first of such clubs in Europe. Tucked away from the main road, the club is very popular with Chiswick residents. As part of the group they also own The Park Club, in Acton.

Opposite: the rather striking yellow house on the corner of Turnham Green and Sutton Court Road.

Above: Corner of Park Road North and Barrowgate Road.

It is interesting to note that as Wikipedia points out, Chiswick Park Station is closer to Turnham Green than the actual station of that name. There has been a station here since 1879 but the current building dates from 1930 when it was rebuilt. The tower was added in order to make the station visible from the High Road.

Chiswick Business Park

Designed by Richard Rogers,
this award-winning business
complex opened in 2002.

Chiswick High Road

Opposite: Chiswick High Road looking west into the late evening sun.

Bottom: After being a regular feature on the High Road for over 40 years, The Ballet Rambert Company is moving to the South bank in December 2013.

Opposite, top right: Carvosso's wine bar and restaurant. This building dates from the 17th century and was converted maintaining many of its original features.

Opposite, bottom: Foster's Bookshop has to be the oldest shop in the High Road; started over 40 years ago by William and Mary Foster as an antique shop; it now just deals in books and is run by their son Stephen (right). He had some fascinating things to tell me; firstly, the window is the original from 1790 and is listed. In the wider area outside his shop used to be a market in the old days, surrounded by pubs, some of which have gone but he told me to look out for the Prince of Wales' feathers above the door to Ladbrokes (below), as that used to be a pub.

Left: This street artist comes from Ealing and is a regular visitor.

Opposite: On the High Road, the statue to Hogarth, by Jim Mathieson, was unveiled in 2001, and was funded by several local benefactors and businesses, and coordinated by the William Hogarth Trust. *www.williamhogarthtrust.org.uk*

Above: The Power House. Following on from the story about the trams in the introduction, this magnificent building provided the energy to drive the trams. The building was rescued and is now Metropolis Music Studios. Set back from the road you could so easily miss it.

Devonshire Road

On the 14th of September 2013, Devonshire Road held their Street Party event. Despite the weather attempting to ruin everything it turned out to be great fun, especially the artists from The Old Saw Theatre Company, who had the audience transfixed with their shortened but hugely entertaining version of Alice in Wonderland (see opposite). The organisers were very pleased as they were able to raise over £1200 for Cancer Recovery – *www.devonshireroadw4.com*

Turnham Green Terrace

Opposite: The corner with Bath Road

Left: Turnham Green Terrace

Right: Turnham Green Tube Station

Chiswick and Turnham Green Terrace still retains some of its more traditional shops, like Mortimer and Bennett, a deli that has been here for over 20 years. A real family affair, Dan Mortimer's nephew, Joe, works behind the counter (left). There is also Macken's the butcher (bottom right), which has been a feature around here for over 50 years. Started by brothers Jim and Peter, Jim's sons Rodney and Jimmy now run the business. That's Damien behind the counter. Then to complete your weekly shop, there is also a traditional fish shop, Covent Garden Fishmongers (top right). Opened by Philip Diamond in 1982, Philip used to be a cab driver and got the name by having started in Covent Garden. They say the high street is struggling and with high rent and rates you can see why that might be but if we want these shops to survive (and let's be honest, these are the kind of craft shops that make any high street), the local community has to make a conscious decision to use them. Let's hope they continue to thrive.

Top: The sign on the side of Oddbin's wine merchants on the corner of Turnham Green Terrace and the High Road. If you look carefully at the photo (top right) you can see the sign on the wall.

A lady enjoying a quiet coffee and a cake at the cafe on the corner of Bath Road – still working you notice with her laptop out.

Opposite, top left: The fountain outside the station.

Opposite, bottom: Maison Blanc.

Right: Turnham Green Terrace looking north.

Churches

Christ Church, Turnham Green. The church dates from 1843 and was funded by public subscription. The church is undergoing some serious renovation as I went to press. Thankfully, I took all the pictures I needed before the scaffolding went up.

St Michael and All Angels in Bedford Park. Designed by Norman Shaw. This church was completed in 1876.

Our Lady of Grace and St Edward; the Catholic Church on Chiswick High Road. Left, as viewed from Dukes Avenue. Opened in 1886, the tower wasn't added until 1930.

Chiswick Parish Church, St Nicholas, Church Street, Old Chiswick. The tower, which dates from the 15th century, is the oldest building in Chiswick.

Top left: Hogarth's tomb.

Left: In the church yard of St. Nicholas can be found many grave stones and memorials to famous local people, amongst them Hogarth of course, but also one to a less well known Italian Ugo Foscolo, who was a highly respected writer and poet. Much effort has been made on the part of the English Italian community to enhance Ugo's resting place, culminating in the recent upgrading of his grave with this impressive memorial.

Right: St. Paul's in Grove Park, which was completed in 1872 and unlike Christ Church, that required the public to help pay for it, St. Paul's was erected by the Duke of Devonshire to serve the new Grove Park community.

Left: St. Michael's Church, Sutton Court, Grove Park, dates from 1909, with its colourful mosaic found by the entrance.

Right: Chiswick Baptist Church, Annandale Road and dates from 1841.

Pubs

Opposite: The Duke of Sussex, now just The Duke, on South Parade, Bedford Park.

Top left and right: The Bulls Head in Strand on the Green.

Bottom: The City Barge in Strand on the Green.

Left: The Station House, by Chiswick Station in Grove Park.

Bottom left: the Tabard in Bath Road, off Turnham Green Terrace.

Bottom: The Crown and Anchor, Chiswick High Road, opposite Turnham Green.

Opposite: The Roebuck on Chiswick High Road.

Fuller's local pubs

Opposite left: The Bell and Crown in Strand on the Green.

Opposite top right: The George IV in the High Road.

Opposite bottom right: The George & Devonshire

Top left: The Duke of York in Devonshire Road.

Bottom left and right: The Fox and Hounds and The Mawson Arms. Situated right beside the brewery, these pubs are combined.

Schools

Opposite and below: Chiswick School, which became an Academy on 2012, is a large secondary school, with over a 1000 pupils. Formed from three local schools, Chiswick County for Boys, Chiswick County for Girls and a secondary modern in Staveley Road; they all came together on the current Burlington Lane site in the early '70s. Interesting to note that Phil Collins, the musician and Genesis singer was a pupil here.

Top right: Grove Park Primary School opened in 1952 on the site formerly owned by St Thomas's Hospital.

Bottom right: Heathfield House School is an independent primary school for boys and girls and was opened in January 2004 in the old Turnham Green Church Hall.

Left: Chiswick and Bedford Park is an independent preparatory school for boys and girls and was established in 1915. Situated in Priory Avenue in the Bedford Park conservation area, the building is Grade II listed.

Top right: The Falcon School for Boys was formerly known as Falkner House and based in Notting Hill. It moved to its present site in Grove Park in 1989 and changed its name to Falcon. It has a sister school for girls in Gunnersbury Avenue.

Bottom right: Belmont Primary School, in Belmont Road behind the High Road has a history stretching back to 1904. Still housed in the original Edwardian building, which is impressive, the school for boys and girls has over 450 pupils.

This page: It's not often that a brand new school opens, especially a secondary school but that's exactly what happened in September 2013 with Kew House, near Strand on the Green and on the approach to Kew Bridge. I have a connection with this school in so much that my children went to their sister school in Ravenscourt Park, hence knowing about it. Although unwell it was good to see Edward Gardener (pictured front row, second from left above) there to officially open the school, a dream of his for some time.

Open Spaces

Chiswick is well endowed with open spaces, some of which are registered common land. The largest of these spaces is Duke's Meadows, which was originally part of the Chiswick House estate. In 1923 the Duke of Devonshire sold 150 acres to Chiswick Urban District Council for £150,000. Chiswick Council subsequently built a riverside promenade with a bandstand and children's playground. Today there are playing fields and sports grounds. Each spring Duke's Meadows provides a wonderful vantage point from which to view the Oxford and Cambridge Boat Race.

In late Victorian times local residents were still grazing horses and geese on Turnham Green. Cricket was played each weekend from the late 19th century to early 21st. On summer weekends local societies hold fêtes and fairs, presenting a colourful scene.

Acton Green is shown as Acton Common on John Rocque's map 1741–5. The common is in South Acton, now within the borough of Ealing, but it is an area that has always looked to Chiswick High Road and the Chiswick underground stations. When the underground line from Turnham Green to Ealing Broadway opened, Chiswick Park Station was called Acton Green, and in 1887 changed to Chiswick Park and Acton Green.

In the 18th century the Green had a few farms, orchards and market gardens along its northern edge. In 1887 St. Alban the Martyr Church was built on the edge of Acton Green. After the railway line was built the area north of the tracks was named Acton Green Common.

Chiswick Common is the area south of the railway line and in the late 19th century was known as 'Back Common'. 'Front Common', meanwhile, was Turnham Green. Each Michaelmas a religious procession from St. Michaels and All Angels church used to make their way across the common. Nowadays a fair visits once a year.

Right: Teasels at Gunnersbury Triangle

Acton Common

Acton Common
incorporated Chiswick
Common until the arrival
of the railway, which
separated them.

Acton Common in spring and summer.

Acton Common looking lovely in all its autumn spendour.

The Fair comes to Acton Common, summer 2013

Chiswick Common

In the middle of Chiswick Common there is a tennis centre with a Routemaster Bus. Not sure what this has to do with tennis but I love these buses. Run by Chris Warren and Liz Bolton, the name Rocks Lane comes from their sister centre in Rocks Lane in Barnes. Although together a long time, they just recently got married, which is nice – congratulations.

Dukes Meadows

Dukes Meadows is the largest of the local open spaces but only because of some campaigning locals and a bit of good fortune. It used to be meadowland owned by the Duke of Devonshire but during the first 20 years of the last century various ideas were floated as to what the land could be used for, from a model village to a gas works. Thankfully nothing happened and in 1923 the Duke sold it to the local council, who decided to keep it open land. In recent times it has become somewhat neglected but a new local group, The Dukes Meadows Trust, is working with the council to try and improve the area, with some success.

Opposite and previous spread: Dukes Meadows can look fabulous in autumn, as it can in winter.

Apart from the open space,
there are many activities that
go on in Dukes Meadows:
sports fields and clubs,
middle left, The Riverside
Club, now part of Virgin.

Dukes Meadows nine-hole golf course.

The Masonians Bowls Club, founded in 1985, is one of the oldest sports clubs on Dukes Meadows and able to trace its history back 1920. I am grateful to their president Terry Pugh, the one in the white cap, who kindly let me join them one summers evening to take these pictures.

At Dukes Meadows there is also a thriving farmers' market every Sunday. You can buy anything from cards, sold by Gill (top right), to meat from Mike the butcher (bottom left), a founder member of the market from when it started 12 years ago.

This spread:
Dukes Meadows
Allotments.

Opposite, bottom right:
Ralph was very proud
of his plot, particularly
his sweetcorn.

Left: Alethea was looking after this plot for a friend. The artichokes were gorgeous.

Opposite: Thank you to Geoff Boswell, seen here with one of his charges, Steven. Geoff very kindly gave his permission for me to take these pictures. He runs a very worthy cause helping adults with learning difficulties. Called Number One Allotment Chiswick Trust, it is a gardening project, which has proven to help adults gain self-confidence and improved quality of life. For more information please visit *www.noact.org.uk*

Gardens

As part of The Bedford Park Festival, the organisers put on an open garden afternoon. Typically the weather didn't play ball but I did ask one or two people if I might come back on a fairer day. This page, thank you to John and Graziella from a house in The Orchard for letting me into their beautiful garden.

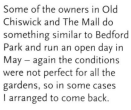

Some of the owners in Old Chiswick and The Mall do something similar to Bedford Park and run an open day in May – again the conditions were not perfect for all the gardens, so in some cases I arranged to come back.

This page: Thank you to Rupert, from along The Mall, for letting me into his garden. His is a newly laid out garden but already the wildlife has taken root and on the day I was there in August, the place was buzzing with insects.

Thank you to Sarah for letting me into her garden, Bedford House, to take these pictures. They have been in it for years but I was interested to hear that it has had some illustrious owners in the past, Michael Redgrave amongst them. Their magnificent magnolia in the front (top right) was planted in 1922.

Thank you to Jane, one of the organisers of the gardens open day, for letting me reproduce these pictures I took on the day in her garden, Swan House.

Gunnersbury Triangle

This is a wonderful little place and on the day I visited I couldn't have been more surprised by the sheer amount of life that I encountered, far too much to record here. The triangle was formed by the onset of the railway lines converging leaving a triangular tract of land somewhat stranded. As recently as the 1980s it was in danger of being sold for development. But due to a local outcry The London Borough of Hounslow were persuaded to buy the land and it is now a designated Local Nature Reserve and managed by the Chiswick Wildlife Group, which is affiliated to the London Wildlife Trust.

Opposite: Bumblebee on a teasel

Top left: The silhouette of a speckled wood butterfly

Top right: A common darter dragonfly

Bottom right: A gatekeeper butterfly

Turnham Green

Turnham Green is registered common land, and is first recorded in 1235 as 'Turneham'. In November 1642 it became the location of the Battle of Turnham Green – an important but non-bloody episode in the Civil War between Charles I's Royalist Army and Cromwell's Parliamentarians. The two sides stood either end of the green in a standoff that lasted about three hours. Short of ammunition and much smaller in number, the Royalist army withdrew after a few shots were fired. Some historians argue that Charles' failure to seize London was pivotal in his ultimate downfall.

Opposite: The wild flower display on Turnham Green this summer was truly spectacular and I was lucky to catch this little girl wandering amongst the daisies.

Above: The blossom was beautiful too.

Turnham Green

The Chiswick Summer Fair is organised and hosted by parishioners of Our Lady of Grace and St. Edwards, Chiswick. Summer 2013 was the 10th anniversary of this popular event and during this time they have raised over £90,000 for local charities.

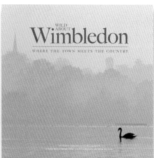
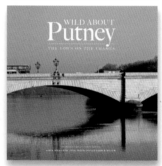

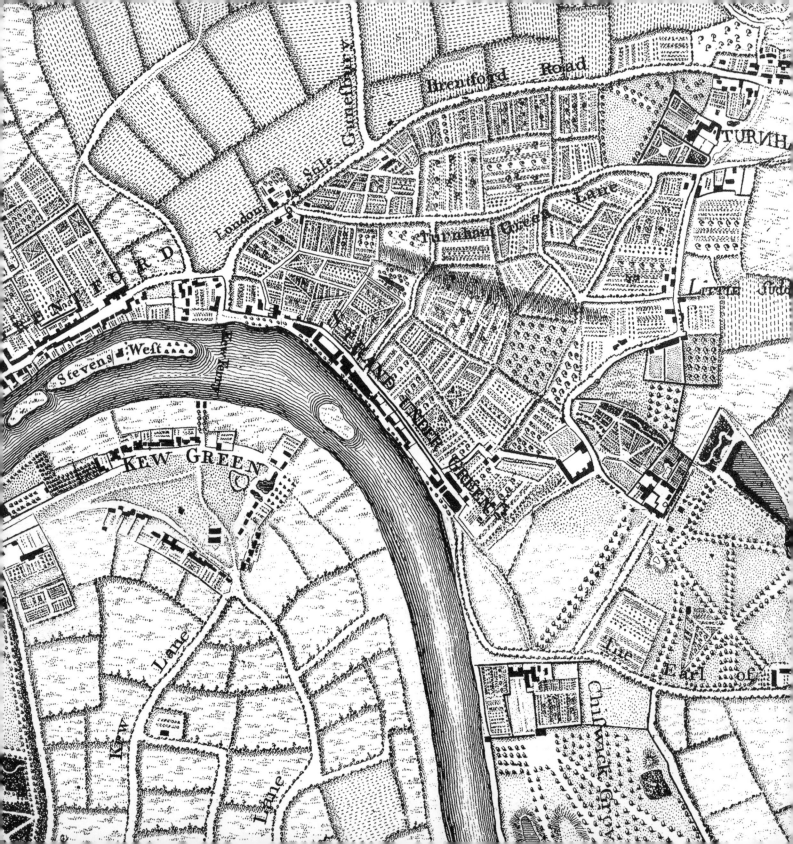

Brentford Road

TURNH

London Stile Gunnersbury

Turnham Green Lane

LANE

LITTLE Studd

FORD

N°

Stevens West

KEW GREEN

NEW GROVE

The Earl of

Kew Lane

Chiswick Grove

Lane